MW00962644

# A Possible Landscape

MAUREEN HARRIS

Brick Books

CANADIAN CATALOGUING IN PUBLICATION DATA

Harris, Maureen, 1943-
A possible landscape

Poems.
ISBN 0-919626-67-X

I. Title.

PS8565.A77P6 1993    C811'.54    C93-095175-1
PR9199.H37P6 1993

We acknowledge the support of the Canada Council for the Arts
for our publishing programme. The support of the Ontario Arts
Council is also gratefully acknowledged.

Cover art is 'Black Jug in Studio Window,' by Josephine Wren, oil
on paper.

Typeset in Ehrhardt. The stock is acid-free Zephyr Antique laid.
Printed and bound by The Coach House Printing Co.

Brick Books
431 Boler Road, Box 20081
London, Ontario
N6K 4G6

www.brickbooks.ca

Thanks to those whose belief in it helped create this book. Particularly implicated are: Lynda Lange, Joe Rosenblatt, Rhea Tregebov, Pat Kennedy, Beverly Clarkson, Peter, Jessica, and Katharine Harris. A special thanks to Marnie Parsons and Sheila Deane, editors extraordinaire, who in more than one instance spied the poem I was trying to write lurking within the one I'd put down on the page.

This one's for Lynda

# Contents

Longing, we say, because desire is full
of endless distances.
Robert Hass, 'Meditation at Lagunitas'

## At the Edge of Winter

Forest – cornstalks – world at the edge
of winter, its light paling as I watch.
Here in the cornfield light dances,
something struggles to take shape.
I'm watching and waiting I don't
know why or what's to happen and

I want to be told into the story,
the one that takes place in the cornfield
at the edge of the forest and winter.
I'll be the one who stands weeping
and the one who goes
head high into the dark, hand out for her lover.

Here is a turning, I shuffle among cornstalks
and trees, saying *ai, ai,* my hair matted,
my hair coiled high above my neck,
I have stumbled into a dance of the old ones
the air sighs its notes in my ear,
and we sway, sway, weaving the dance
weaving cornstalks among pines,
praising the one who has gone
the one who'll return.

# A Narrow Room

## Invocation

I am being held here in the body.
*That* is the meaning of stone.
Snake-mother teach me to shed
eyes     hair     skin
till I reach bright bone.

Lady unnamed not nameless
in the labyrinth of the skull
lead me to remember
passage and joining
till I hear words grow full.

*That Strange Sense of Falling*


I dream of tunnels into the earth, of rolling
from the top of a high cliff slowly tilting
over to splash resoundingly
into sea.

Walking through puddles I grow dizzy.
Surfaces open out into nothing
to stand on, whatever is flat heaves
slightly, corners gape, bridges are fluid.
What dissolves is

distance, edges, my hand
reaching out

## *Eve Again*

Poor rib.
Only a piece of dumb bone
a curve circling his heart,
protecting it.

A raw beginning –
A stiff silence

## The Garden

The air in the garden is alive.
It is merely sunshine,
sensuous on skin,
and clear, so clear it is unseen
but felt as light breathing,
air taking in air.

## Let Me

Let me turn away from you, let me
leave remembering the way my
skin blossoms beneath your touch –

Frangipani, oleander, trumpet
vines climb around me.
I am your jungle garden,
tangle of paths, secret openings,
unexpected pools.

I stumble, lost among flowers
don't know which way to turn.

## Snick Snick

1   'Look before you bite'
the snake's last words ...
he flopped, choking
in the dust.

'Too late, too late'
I hissed
apple on my chin,
reaching for a second skin
to pull around me.

2   Nibbles, nibbles my earlobe.
The *snick snick snick*
of his tongue nips a notch
where beads of blood
and venom glitter.

With a whirr he uncoils,
drops, trails about my ankles.
The sweet bite sings sings
at the base of my skull.

## Snake in the Grass

I half-expect that green fellow
to sashay up
shedding his skin with a snap
rise beside me and
unzip me with his tongue
till I glimmer like marshfire
flickering through the apple trees.

## The Mother of Us All

wiped her forehead
Cain's nose
Abel's face
Seth's bottom
pitched the boys outside
to play in the farmyard.

She yelled at her no-name daughters
to quit messing in the dirt
and go tidy their rooms.
Cursed Adam
gone to town
three days now.

The mother of us all
leaned against her tree, sighed
for the snake, his green quiver,
his sibilant caress, his
supple tongue that promised
a different Paradise.

## Some Snakes Travel in Pairs

Never fall in love with a snake;
he's subtle and sloughs off fidelity.
Never fall in love with a snake;
he'll soon tire of your wearing
the same skin day-out, day-in.

*Personals*

Princess in tower
    waiting to be found

Prince seeking princess
    equally spellbound

## A Narrow Room
for Susan Mitchell

1  You asked for everything.
Conversation, food from my plate,
a place on my pillow –

The only thing *I* ever wanted
was space, a chance to
step beyond your voice
to see the world
without relaying it to you,
to touch a leaf, a stone wall
without bruising my hand.

Finally I gave you rage
like a geyser arcing
you through the air
to clatter against the wall
and fall like a pebble to
the floor.

You were born again of that anger
and as you clambered to your feet
even the shape of your face had changed.

Now you spend your time walking
by the river talking to strangers
and I'm still waiting for
the word that will unleash me.

2   Once again you've gone,
    the sharp slap of your boots
    on the stairs grows muffled.
    You near the base of the tower, slide
    into the well's black water;
    I drown in solitude.

    I'm possessed by images of you
    eluding my glance, slipping
    from body to body
    neither prince nor frog.
    I dream of you:
    a flash of gold
    disappearing into the well,
    crease of pain across my chest,
    salt taste of tears,
    the sound of your voice.

    Now the days speak salt.
    I wake to find gold hair on your pillow, miss
    that smooth green self you were.

    Rage in my throat, my
    fists hammering
    these stone walls.

3   Restive as water in sunlight
    as the shifting world he ponders,
    his thoughts circle.
    Surrounded by air he founders.

    His fingers
    twitch to grow longer,
    webbed, ready to cup water.
    He dreams of legs thrusting with power.

    I watch him for hours staring after
    some hint of shape in which he could be at home
    where thought and gesture meld with one another
    and he plies this world simply
    as he once did water.


4   Happily ever after
    is a narrow room
    with crisp white borders.
    No voices spill over the edge.

    Slowly we close those covers
    and crawl into bed.
    There is little to be said.
    We have only the silence
    scratching his chest and yawning
    like an ordinary man home from work
    wanting his usual drink, his usual paper.

## The Frog Prince Revisited

If I could imagine you here,
not bound by the page's edge
or that stone well but with
your feet ankle-deep in
marsh marigolds on the creek bank
the riffle of sunlight down
through these particular trees
maple   oak   birch   not fully-
leafed yet, cedar scenting
the air, that dim cloud of
insects winding about your head,
rusty cry of blackbirds from
the marsh where cattails stand
browned and scruffy still –

\*

Not what I expected:
this ordinary man
leaving wet footprints as he walks.

## Brooch

The frog is sunlight not water
two gold legs reaching out
as if it would climb
the shoulder on which it is pinned.

Not green but gold
it hovers on the verge
of disappearance
urging me to hold on
to cup my hands round it
and once again carry him home.

## The Wicked Queen's Story

You swallow nothing. What I feed you
sticks in your throat as if I schemed
to end the story here
with us glaring across the table
voices raised, fists clenched.

You follow the huntsman into the forest,
drawn by his broad shoulders and lean haunches.
You don't see that this is only the beginning
of another story: drudgery, lonely days
at the beck and call of whoever mends the roof
over your head or brings home the venison.

He's a prince, you say, come to carry you
to your own kingdom far from our clamour.
You don't believe there is anything but
'happily ever after.'

You can't know
how short a time
is the reign of the true queen.

You were curled, here, beneath my heart.
But you won't believe that story either.
Though I stretch my arms out to you and dance
I am no match for your clear white dreams,
your red passion, your black hatred.

## Persephone's Dream

I descend the staircase
beside the stone wall
and clamber over the scattered brick lintel
to stop and stare across the meadow.

Here. Here is where it happened.
The earth split open, the slide to darkness began –
that team of four black horses rearing,
that god in armour, his burning black eyes.
I don't remember any sounds,
not even my own voice screaming.

In the meadow flowers dance
but I don't lean to pick them;
I'm alone except for a solitary crow
flying past. I walk through grass
glittering in sunlight but never reach
the trees on the other side
leaves full of voices.

Then it was only sound,
my name echoing harshly from earth to sky,
rattling through the dark corridors
till I longed to stop my own ears
and couldn't tell who called, or why.

I try these stairs again
thinking to find my own way down
but it is always the meadow and empty and
reverberating with my name.
    As if someone had just left

## Alice

*What* was I looking for? –
this flat place, this quiet lake,
a porcelain dish in the middle of
hills, a state of mind, a mirror?
Nothing seemed to fit the bill.
My hand curled, uncurled.

It was only a dream. A brick path leading
towards the river and there was nothing
plain in the garden, rings
of hedges, clipped box,
petunias curled over wire frames, those
curved and frightened branches,
blood-red roses in formal beds.

Nothing was signed and the sun was hidden
so we moved in any direction carried
on the wash of flowers.
I wanted to lie down on a bench and
drum my heels furiously. I wanted
to trade hands with the gardener.

## Hermes

It's cold on this hilltop
with snow blowing around.
Your torch glimmers.
I can scarcely see your crook.

The flock huddles together
for warmth by the fold.
They want the gate to be opened.

I thought I knew another gate.
I wanted to say 'journey,' 'border,'
'transformation,' 'gemstone,'
'dragon.' I thought I'd begin
speaking of something grand –

But truth is I stepped backwards
avoiding your hand,
teetered off the rock,
and fell into the arms of some rough fool
wearing sheepskin and burlap,
laughing uproariously.

# Where Things Come Together

## Where Things Come Together
for Richard Howard, for Michael Palmer

In this country there's no telling.
White hands swoop by the window, trees bend.
Who knew that marble could bring warmth?
Float out of darkness and gesture?
Distracting me –

He spoke of boundaries and partitions,
periodizing history to hold (grasp) it,
cutting it up to understand.

I imagine my hand lying on a glass table,
the drapes silk, pale green and gold.
A painting hangs on the wall
opposite a drawing by Rodin.
It is 1933 and the room is empty
but at any moment –

Naming is another way to hang (hold) on to (something).
Richard or Michael, I say, knowing neither of them.
I have seen what they say. Listen –

along the wall the paintings rub shoulders.
People sit outside a café, lights flash,
stars rain down from the sky, there is music.
The corner turns and I face a field.
The road doesn't reach the horizon.

And in this country there's no speaking
the picture moves so quickly through the frame.
It recedes till it lies at the end of a long hallway.
Or, it rises till it's lost in the sky.
At any moment I can't see it anymore.
A hand gropes (for the wall).

At any moment I see the hallway or the sky.
The white hands are stopped time
like a film cut into a series of stills.
We turn them over, insist on their motion.
Emotion recollected in tranquillity.
A unity in fragments, he said.

What I meant to tell you.
Naming is another way to hand on.
In this country anything

## Crossing the Bar
for Jane Urquhart

Annie Oakley taps her way across the floor,
places her hand on the edge of the bar,
leaps onto it lightly. The piano player
cocks his hat and the music begins.
We raise our bottles high in time
and while we sing Annie dances
from one end of the bar to the other.

Outside it's dark and the water laps
at the edge of the sidewalk
and we might have come from anywhere,
might have been found
stepping into or out of a boat
docking slowly by a brick embankment.

And oh the sparkle and the splendour
of bottles of coloured liquors,
of glasses before gilt mirrors.
Laughing, arms linked in a circle,
we sway and sing, heads nearly touching
and where have we been where have we been
where can we go by music and water?

Outside it's dark and a boat bumps the sidewalk
in time to the wash of the music
and we might have come by water
murmuring the names of places we might have seen
as we stared into the dark for a landing.

Annie crosses the bar in her high-heeled tap shoes,
our glasses rattling to their rhythm,
and where we might have been we scarcely know
as whispers from the dark rock us.
The boat may leave at any moment
the circle widening, and who will remember
the sound of water outside the music
what it meant, the scent of the night air?

## The Way I Wish It Was

July. The days are long and I am away.
The sky is luminous, there is space everywhere.
Letters heap up in my mailbox. Stieglitz has not
photographed me but he continues to write.
He likes my poems, he says, keep on.
There is no one I need talk to through the long afternoons.

My book will be called *A Woman on Paper*.
On its cover will be a picture I took
of the opening horizon, sky piled up over a field.
It may have rained once a while ago.
Georgia O'Keeffe has just spoken to me.
*Look*, she said, and I turn

## Occasional Letters
for Rhea Tregebov

'Occasional letters, written to the moment, may provide a temporary
role, but they threaten to erode any confidence that the self may be
more than the accumulation of its various roles ...'
                Francis Ferguson, 'The Unfamiliarity of Familiar Letters'

'We outlive, not ourselves, but our succession of selves.'
                Joyce Carol Oates, *The Assignation*

1   I want you to know I did not dream this up.
    There I stood at the corner, upright as could be,
    when my umbrella blew inside-out.
    Why make up such a story?
    The foolishness of it
    rain running down my back
    and me holding my startled umbrella to the sky –
    Mary Poppins gone wrong.
    In the rush of traffic, my old black coat blowing,
    can you imagine how I felt?
    My arm reaching to the end of the umbrella
    and water splashing out of the gutter as cars turned,
    I was wet and embarrassed,
    a cartoon character, slapstick.

    And suddenly it all ran backwards.

    The water fell away from my coat hem back into the gutter,
    the black tulip of my umbrella majestically unfurled,
    and with a mighty shout I was aloft
    sailing serenely above the traffic
    out of the rain and into blue sky,
    the city receding beautiful beneath me.

    Let me tell you,
    things look very different
    from up here.

2  By now of course you're grinning
   and shaking your head –
   'What a pity she gave in,
   just when it was getting interesting.'

   I suppose that's true.
   The ascent is simple enough
   but it beats me to think of hovering there
   indefinitely, rain or shine, day and night.
   My arm gets tired when I think about it.
   So I'm down to earth again and I
   never did tell you how things looked
   from up there.


3  The question now is
   why you should believe I'm down to earth again
   sober, sedate, completely
   trustworthy.

   Well, take a look.

   I carry a black briefcase
   never an umbrella
   and my shoes are elegantly sensible.
   I never mount staircases, climb hills,
   or take elevators to the tops of tall buildings.
   I make my bed before I leave in the morning,
   put the cereal box back in the cupboard,
   never run out of milk.
   I buy cut flowers once a week
   and ask a neighbour for dinner.
   I've stopped worrying about how I look,
   about getting the story straight.

4   I was wrong again,
    caught up in another tall tale
    of not scaling the heights,
    enthralled by matching shoes and briefcase,
    the serviceable trim of them.
    The tale told itself smoothly enough
    but grew dull.

    One evening I fell asleep
    and the next morning there I was –
    down-at-heel, the handle of my briefcase broken,
    and a pile of dog-eared papers in my hand:
    unanswered letters, unwritten poems,
    a torn invitation to the next space launch
    (the ship to be manned by women and dolphins;
    date and place missing).

    I go walking in the rain a lot now,
    holding my umbrella,
    kicking my way through piles of sodden leaves,
    and checking the newspaper boxes
    for a headline about the launch.
    Next time the wind comes up
    I'll be ready.

5   Those dolphins
    browse white as the moon
    at the edges of islands,
    know about travelling deep.

    Caught in the shoals of the self
    in November rain
    barefoot, my umbrella lost
    I wish for companions
    at ease in the ocean.


6   All this up and down,
    this toying with notions of travel,
    as if I had to go somewhere else
    to see where I am.

    I expect you've half-heard
    the breaks in syntax, the gaps between words.
    Perhaps I tripped on my own umbrella
    and had to pick myself up
    chagrined, brushing bits of dirt from my legs, pretending
    I'm fine, nothing happened.

    Has anyone seen me?

## Travel Journal
for Dagmar

Fields speak as she speeds by.
Trees' gossip rises and falls round
a steadier tone: columns of air sigh.
The roads chatter while these low
hills hum their own tunes.

Her sounds penetrate the landscape –
clatter of motor, stutter of wheels,
all muffled inside the helmet
her pulse in her ears.

Landscape, motorcycle, pulse
join voices.

Rounding a corner pause and listen:
she hears herself vanishing

> Each evening she sits
> notebook on knee
> describing the road
> that fell behind.
> She remembers
> travelling cocooned
> in sounds, unwinds them
> one by one: re-
> collecting the landscape
> as she does herself,
> determined to find
> that single voice
> she dreams her own.

## As If I Didn't Live Here Anymore

The green lawn beyond my doorway
is distant, foreign, empty of memories.
An envelope of silence presses in
wrinkling about me as I move.
Sometimes I hear words no one has spoken.

It's not that I can't pick up my cup
but this coffee tastes of elsewhere and
there is no hand on my breast.
There is no one at all here

the flavour of possibility,
the sharpest sensation in the room.

## Desire

Alone in the cluttered room with
only a tattered poster and the wall of
family photographs staring blankly ahead
to witness I shred your drawing
into bite-sized pieces and eat them
silently, one by one, a private sacrament,
body only, here is your body, piece by
piece I chew them slowly, carefully.
Sitting on the edge of my bed I swallow
you piece by piece. The drawing,
the last shred chewed and swallowed,
is gone. I lie down in my bed and pull
the sheet up over my head. Knees drawn
up to my chin in the dark hollow,
feeling you inside me, all those little
chewed-up pieces of you inside me circu-
lating throughout my body filling me. I
contain you piece by piece in the darkness
you flow through me and now here in the
darkness alone in the darkness I will
never be hungry again.

## Cutting Cards

To let down some image of myself, dangling,
the hanged woman, head lolling, tongue out,
feet splayed from the last faint dancing shudder –
creak of wood, screel of unwinding chain,
and the long fall to underground water
where something descends, sinks –

To let down some image of myself
cut myself free from what I meant to be,
half-minded, half-minding what I was told,
hobbling one-footed along the corridor
my hands full of whatever I've been handed,
my neck so stiff I couldn't turn it
to glimpse the window.

To let down some image of myself,
meaning, really, to fail.
To lay to rest this heavy likeness,
to cut loose the dead weight, feet dangling,
and let it drop like a stone to the well's bottom.

I've laid it out, shut her eyes with old coin,
rubbed oil in the crease on her forehead,
muttered something pedestrian, prayed for luck.
May she be silent. May she rest,
undisturbed. May words always bless her and intervene
against her resurrection.

## *Emblem*

There is no moment at which I am not going somewhere
the door still swinging shut behind me I am looking sideways
there is a curb and across the road there is another
and for ten minutes now I've been on my way in a par-
ticular direction when the street shifts and runs uphill.
At the intersection I half-look both ways the door has
closed now but the window is open and a trail skirts the
bottom of the hill (from behind it I hear voices) I am
carrying a cup of coffee in my hand my fingers
are sticky I was supposed to turn left at the hill I
was supposed to be home by six p.m. but the door has
clicked shut and there is no window at the curve in the trail
only a choice of directions and I am going some
how at every moment I am still going on somewhere –
There is no moment in which I am standing still.

*Self-Portrait:*
*My Extraverted Life Spreads Out in Front of Me*

and my desk struggles to bear up manfully
beneath its invisible projects
each dreaming its way towards completion,
a rich fantasy of perfect endings.
The desk hungers to neaten, to find itself light
beneath precise and actual words
heavy with significance.
                              But here *I* am
turning towards the always-open door.
'Yes' I say 'Of course' I say 'I can do that.'
Smiling I add on whatever is asked of me,
this balancing, extending, a charming challenge.

I am busy with conversations in the elevator,
how the weather changes, the air thickening,
the continual approach of new possibilities
looking for someone to acknowledge them.
So-and-so is sick, there's a stranger here,
someone's mother is dying, we're all tired by three p.m.,
no-one answers the phone, I run to it,
where's my pencil, I'll make the coffee,
did you get the message?, god will the rain *ever* end?

But when the door closes and the heat's off
the elevator I enter goes down slantwise
angling through tunnels of deep blue fabric –
its walls shift and curve, it seems to breathe,
beyond it are valleys, a possible landscape.
There must be silence, though my head spins from it.
If I breathe slowly enough I'll find my way down
past this unease and stepping through a curtain
I find meadow grass, a heap of words, shimmering.

## An Unnaming: the Ottawa

From this high hotel window I watch the river
broad and stippled, dull silver under clouds and evening.

Trees reclaim the landscape, pushing over buildings,
bruising windows and bursting concrete in dreamy silence
while small cries of unknown birds pierce the air.

It's morning and I'm stiff from sleeping on the ground.
The only direction I know is where the sun rose spearing
me awake and I can name nothing here but flat shapes
against the sky:    blossom    leaf    bird    branch    river.

## The Private Lives of Transit Drivers

The young man with truck-driver-long hair curling round his shoulders
slouches slightly back against his chair, the uniform editing his
    movements
so that only his hand lumbering us round this awkward Oakwood corner
    swaggers.
Day after day the grid of streets, and there just aren't enough young
    women
with silky hair who smile and chat, leaning towards him from their
    seats.

This morning the man with the pointed beard and blurred Van Dyck
    face
is sullen. His hand has thought of something it dropped a long time ago.
The smell of fresh banana stretches out through the swaying streetcar
and I'm remembering a driver I saw once, hair rumpled, shoulder
    against the window,
looking us over as he pulled an empty train into the St. Clair West
    station
and dreaming the temptation to drive it fast straight through
barrelling down the thin bright track and out the far end of the tunnel.

## The Herdsman's Children
for Michael Hulse

*April 15, 1991.*
Every day and the world spills in on me when what I want to do
is think about drowning, the meaning of going under, the great below.

Nineteen small bundles lined up today in the mosque morgue at
    Jucurdja Camp
and it's raining here as well as there, though the sound here is only
sparrow argument and not the stretched-thin wailings of small hungers.

The children are in line at the edge of the world where we've placed
    them.

I stand with my face to the window, mouth open.
The daffodils push and push towards blossom against the rain and
    nineteen
cloth-wrapped bundles line up behind them where a widening passage
gapes and gapes and I don't want to know about
this way of going under opening among daffodils in my garden.

                            *

*March 1992.*
Remembering myself at the window: hands gripping the back of a chair,
daffodils, rain, the precision of cold glass on my forehead
representing the wails of dying children.

We lean towards these sensations, the focus of them,
this limited connection. Watching the dying, several worlds away,
the pulse curves, then steadies, as we stutter towards words, stammer
    outrage,
anguish (mean it, every single word of it), never,
our tongues taut, loosening our throats and unleashing the animal howl,
that inarticulate rough sound, the body's unlearned untidy response.

At the edge of the world the children

## The Woman at the Bottom of the Well

                              is silent,
hopes never to open her mouth again against
the fatigue, the weight of all she has said pulling
her to the dark pebbled shore where the reeds
curve over and even the reflection
of the moon is partial.
She longs for no opening out of the dark,
blessing the thick tongue, the undisturbed hollows
of her ears, the still vocal chords, all those parts of herself
complicit with silence.

## What Is Lost Now
for Bronwen Wallace

The women rise up for death.
Inclining a little forward they
adjust their cloaks, arms
gently pulling the air about them.

They've come without thought
knowing the sounds that are proper,
that issue from the bone to declare
what is lost now to dirt, wash of rain.

The women's voices sound her slow turn
towards the doorway between oak trees,
that absence we have glimpsed,
figure of emptiness where she stood.

## *Winter Dark, Wind Rattling the House*

The long fingers of winter tug at my dreams
pulling me off balance, insistent, constant, trying
to turn my head and force me to look,
to meet darkness eye-to-eye and see full-face
the forgotten and discarded parts of myself.

Oh, if you look, darkness lies in our ears,
pools up in smudges below our eyes,
trips out on the tips of our tongues,
will not go away, does not dissolve in sunlight,
but only gathers itself behind leaves,
along edges of gnarled tree-roots,
then rushes to meet the soles of our feet descending.

Turning my face towards the darkness
I encounter what is lost, what is gathering itself
beneath winter's snow, to be born

## Spring

How can I render the meaning of sunlight
on this red brick wall
spreading its warm fingers wide,
the open palm of the world where time passes,
pauses for a moment to bask, moves on again?

This dappling of shadows on warm stone,
their blurred and shifting patterns
playing across brick's smudged geometry,
the pale warmth of spring sunshine after days of rain,
lighting up kitchen, backyard, the whole street,
so we all stop for a moment,
lift our heads from what we're doing,
and stand musing, caught at the season's edge,
the turning visible and true.

*Travelling by Eye*

Following this route, the one for the eye,
I am carried by light in its variations
over the crest of a green hill.
On the other side I have imagined
dense forest.
    What the eye tells
is of movement – the dance of leaves
glinting in sunlight, pale
beige cornstalks which do not move
though the light does, and they seem to.

Following the eye out through light,
through colour, through all those dancing leaves,
I find the world, feasting us.

*An Answer*

What this woman wants is a different
life, one with darkness glowing
in its green heart glossy
and thick-veined as a leaf.

The birds nestle in the bush, silent,
waiting for words of twilight calling, calling.

Voices of frogs in the dark, cool tongues of
water, a world within the world. The taste of it.

BARBARA KERSLAKE

Since the original publication of *A Possible Landscape*, Maureen Scott Harris has published a chapbook, *The World Speaks* (Junction Books) and a second collection of poems, *Drowning Lessons* (Pedlar Press), which was awarded the 2005 Trillium Book Award for Poetry in English. She lives in Toronto and has been production manager of Brick Books since 2001.